INDONESIA
A NATION OF ISLANDS

DISCOVERING our HERITAGE

By Judy Jacobs

DILLON PRESS, INC.
Minneapolis, Minnesota 55415

Acknowledgments

This book would not have been possible without the help of many people. I'd like to thank Lora Lee Polack, my editor at Dillon Press; my husband Mihaly Kun; and my son Joshua.

Thanks also to all those who answered my endless questions: Johannes and Melanie Tan, Halim and Marlianty Indrakusuma, Sri Jasmeini Mudji Dachri, Mrs. Dh Kadar, John Susanto, Anwar Rawy, Sofyan Jusuf, Nico Pasaka, Gusti Bagus Yudhara, Mrs. Nokorda Raka Sukawati, the teachers and principals of S.D. Latihan and S.D. Menteng Dalam #12, Titi Utami Johannes, Rusman Hadi Santosa, Wayne Vitale, Larry Reed, John Senduk, Mary Louise Totton, Jeff Kaliss, Emil Mailengky, Isran Budianto, and Suzanne Suwanda.

Photographs have been reproduced through the courtesy of Phyllis Elving, Bonnie Kamin, Barbara Zang, Richard Bangs, George Fuller, Dave Heckman, Lawrence Burr, Jim Slade, the Indonesian Photo Service, Antara, Pacific Discoveries, Pacific Asia Travel Association, and Select Tours International. Cover photo by Barbara Zang.

Library of Congress Cataloging-in-Publication Data

Jacobs, Judy.
    Indonesia : a nation of islands / by Judy Jacobs.
      p.   cm. — (Discovering our heritage)
    Includes bibliographical references.
    Summary: Examines the history, people, politics, culture, and major cities of Indonesia.
    ISBN 0-87518-423-5 (lib. bdg.) : $12.95
    1. Indonesia—Juvenile literature. [1. Indonesia.] I. Title.
II. Series.

DS615.J23   1990
959.8—dc20   89-29213
                                                CIP
                                                  AC

Dillon Press, Inc., 242 Portland Avenue South
Minneapolis, Minnesota 55415

Printed in the United States of America
1 2 3 4 5 6 7 8 9 10 99 98 97 96 95 94 93 92 91 90

Contents

Fast Facts about Indonesia

Official Name: Republic of Indonesia

Capital: Jakarta

Location: Indonesia is an island nation located in the sea off the southeastern coast of Asia. It consists of 13,677 islands, which stretch eastward from the Malay Peninsula to the sea north of Australia

Area: 741,101 square miles (1,919,443 square kilometers). *Greatest distances:* east-west—about 3,200 miles (5,150 kilometers); north-south—about 1,200 miles (1,930 kilometers)

Elevation: *Highest*—Mount Puncak Jaya on Irian Jaya, at 16,503 feet (5,030 meters) above sea level. *Lowest*—sea level along the coasts

Population: 176,000,000 (1989 estimate). *Distribution*—75 percent rural, 25 percent urban. *Density*—233 persons per square mile (90 per square kilometer). About 60 percent of the people live on the island of Java, which has a density of about 1,788 persons per square mile (690 per square kilometer)

Form of Government: Republic. *Head of Government*—President

Important Products: *Mining*—oil, natural gas, coal, nickel, tin, bauxite, iron ore. *Forest Industry*—lumber. *Agriculture*—rice, palm oil, rubber, copra, sugar, coffee, tea, pepper, tobacco

Basic Unit of Money: Rupiah

Official Language: Bahasa Indonesia

Major Religions: More than 80 percent of all Indonesians are Muslims. Other religions recognized by the government are Hinduism, Protestantism, Catholicism, and Buddhism

Flag: A field that is divided horizontally into two equal halves; the upper half is red and the lower is white

National Anthem: *Indonesia Raya* ("Indonesia the Great")

Major Holidays: Independence Day (August 17). Other holidays vary depending on the person's religion or ethnic group—Muslims celebrate Hari Raya, which marks the end of the fasting month and falls on a different date each year; Christians celebrate Christmas on December 25; the Hindus of Bali celebrate Galungan every 210 days

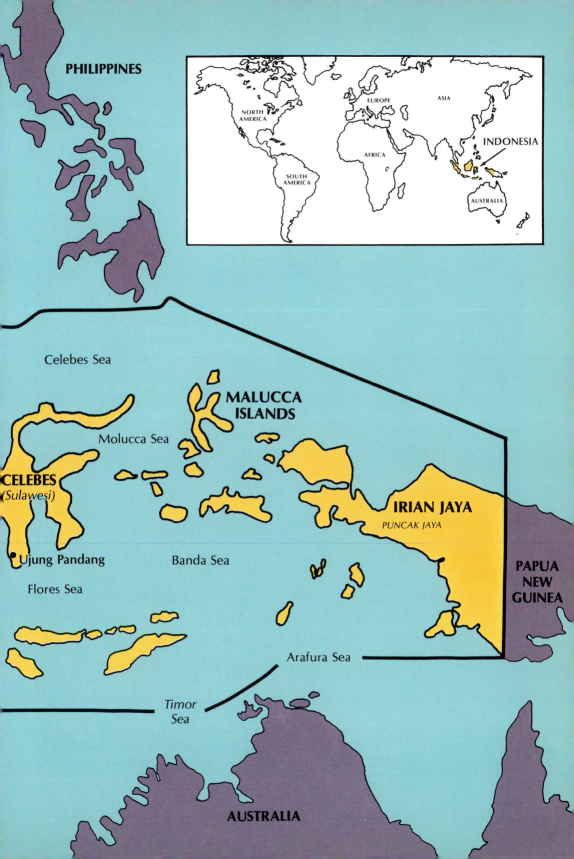

PHILIPPINES

NORTH
AMERICA

EUROPE

ASIA

INDONESIA

AFRICA

SOUTH
AMERICA

AUSTRALIA

Celebes Sea

MALUCCA
ISLANDS

Molucca Sea

CELEBES
(Sulawesi)

IRIAN JAYA

PUNCAK JAYA

• Ujung Pandang

Banda Sea

PAPUA
NEW
GUINEA

Flores Sea

Arafura Sea

Timor
Sea

AUSTRALIA

In North Sumatra, farmers make their way to market to sell their produce.

1. Islands in the Sea

Spread out over more than thirteen thousand islands, Indonesia is a land of great variety. In the jungle of one island, a tattooed tribeswoman slowly paddles a canoe upstream in search of fish for her family's dinner. On another island, a young girl arranges a flower offering for the Hindu gods before she leaves for school down a path between brilliant green rice fields. In a large city on a third island, a reporter waits in his car in a traffic tie-up, on his way to the television studio where he broadcasts the news by satellite. In a small town on still another island, Muslim families are awakened by the sound of a loudspeaker calling them to prayer.

The island nation of Indonesia includes tiny fishing villages, bustling cities, fields carved out of mountainsides, smoking volcanoes, beaches lined with swaying palm trees, and much more. Nearly 350 different ethnic groups live in the islands, each with its own language, culture, and way of life. Some are modern city dwellers, while others live in a way that has not changed much in thousands of years.

The islands of Indonesia are located in the sea to the south and east of mainland Southeast Asia. Indonesia stretches for more than 3,000 miles (4,830 kilometers) eastward from Malaysia, to near the coast of Australia. The Indian Ocean washes the shores of many of the southernmost islands, while the Philippines lies directly to the north of others.

With more than 170 million people, Indonesia is the largest nation in Southeast Asia. It ranks fifth in population among all the nations of the world. Because more than 80 percent of its people are Muslim, Indonesia is also the largest Muslim country on earth.

Thousands of Islands

The 13,677 islands of Indonesia are spread out over an area that is wider than the United States. Most of this area is water, though—the Indonesian people even call their country *Tanah Air Kita*, which means "our land and water."

Many of the islands are very small, covering less than 1 square mile (2.6 square kilometers). Some of them are not inhabited. Yet Indonesia also contains portions of two of the world's largest islands. The nation shares the island of Borneo with the countries of Malaysia and Brunei—Indonesia's two-thirds of Borneo is known as Kalimantan. Half of the island of New Guinea belongs to Indonesia—it is called Irian Jaya. The other half is a separate nation known as Papua New Guinea.

On crowded Java, almost all of the available land is used to grow crops.

Of the islands that belong completely to Indonesia, the three largest are Sumatra, Java, and Sulawesi. Sumatra, the largest and westernmost, is near Malaysia. Java is separated from Sumatra by the narrow Sunda Strait. Sulawesi lies to the northeast from Java.

The most important smaller island is Bali, located only five miles (eight kilometers) east of Java. To the northeast lies a group of islands called the Moluccas. During the sixteenth century, these islands supplied valuable spices to Europe and were at the center of a struggle between many nations who sought to control this trade.

About six of every ten Indonesians live on Java, making this island one of the most crowded places on earth. Java is so crowded that it is not unusual for thirty or forty people to work side-by-side planting rice in a field. Nearby Bali is also crowded, with about three million people squeezed onto the small island. On other Indonesian islands, though, there are vast, forested areas with few people living in them.

About two out of every three Indonesians earn their living from the land. Most farmers grow rice, but in the highlands they grow corn and sweet potatoes. Some raise cloves and other spices or coffee to earn money for luxuries such as motorcycles or televisions. Many also keep chickens for eggs and a goat or two for milk.

Jakarta is a busy, modern city.

Indonesia also has several large cities. The largest and most important, Jakarta, is located on Java. With more than six million residents, it is the country's capital and business center. In this sprawling city, the traditional and modern exist side-by-side. High-rise buildings tower over quiet neighborhoods of whitewashed homes with tile roofs. At Jakarta's port, workers unload lumber from wooden sailing ships and automobiles from modern cargo freighters.

Most of the country's other major cities are also seaports. Surabaya, located on the north coast of Java,

In many parts of Indonesia, people are more likely to travel by boat than by bus.

is Indonesia's second largest city and an important naval center. Two other port cities are Medan in Sumatra and Ujung Pandang in Sulawesi. Denpasar is the largest city on Bali.

The seas between the islands are important in the daily life of the people. These seas—which include the Java Sea, Celebes Sea, and Molucca Sea—supply fish for the people to eat and are the main "roads" between the islands. Most Indonesians travel by boat, and many earn a living by trading between the nation's hundreds of small ports.

Since the Indonesian islands lie along the equator, the temperature remains nearly the same for most of the year. The weather is hot and tropical, with a rainy season on most islands lasting from December through March. On some days, it rains so hard that many people do not even leave their homes. City dwellers who do may have to struggle through flooded streets which have turned into small rivers.

A Land of Volcanoes

Most of the islands of Indonesia are mountainous. Irian Jaya is home to snow-capped peaks, such as the 16,503-foot (5,030-meter) Puncak Jaya, the highest mountain in Southeast Asia. Java and Sumatra both have mountain ranges running from one end to the other. Mountain peaks rise in the center of Bali.

Indonesia also has many volcanoes. Some are still active, spouting smoke into the air and occasionally causing the earth to tremble. The country's most famous volcano, Krakatoa, can be found in the ocean off the tip of western Java. In 1883, Krakatoa erupted with enormous force—the largest explosion in modern history. The boom could be heard in Australia, more than 2,000 miles (3,220 kilometers) away. Eighty years later, Gunung Agung erupted on Bali, sending lava and cinders across the eastern half of the island and killing

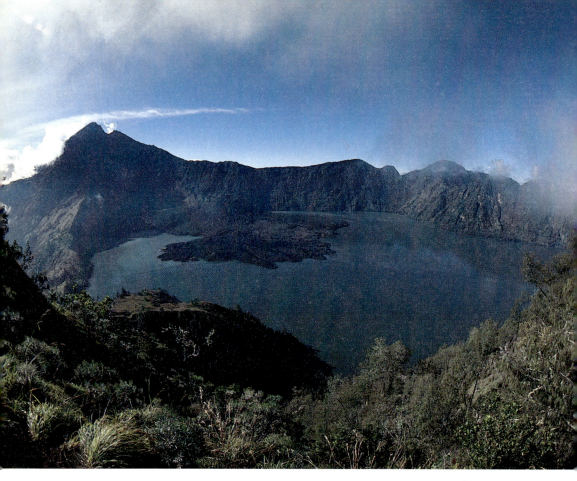

*Like many Indonesian volcanoes, the crater of Mount Rinjani
has become a lake.*

more than 1,500 people. Today, many parts of eastern
Bali still resemble a gray, ashen desert.

Although Indonesia's volcanoes cause much de-
struction, the volcanic ash they produce adds rich nu-
trients to the soil, making the land very fertile. On Java
and Bali, the soil is so rich that the Javanese claim a
banana tree can grow in ten weeks. Farmers on these
islands usually harvest two or three rice crops a year.

Many volcanoes that are no longer active have

beautiful lakes in their craters. Keli Mutu on the island of Flores has three crater lakes in three different colors: blue, red, and green. The people of Flores say that these lakes have changed colors over the years. According to scientists, the colors are caused by minerals in the lake water.

Rain Forests and Dragons

On crowded Java and Bali, most of the land has been cleared to make rice fields. Farmland is so valuable that even the mountains have been used, with fields carved like steps up the sides. Yet more than 80 percent of the land on the other islands is covered with a thick, tropical rain forest. The tallest trees in these forests reach more than 150 feet (46 meters) in height.

Because it is divided into so many islands, Indonesia has a wide variety of plant life, including hundreds of species of palm trees, bamboo, and flowers such as orchids, hibiscus, and frangipani. Some Indonesian plants are very unusual. The rafflesia, the world's largest flower, can grow wider than 3 feet (.9 meter) across. The corpse plant smells like a dead animal, but the smell attracts insects that help pollinate it.

Some Indonesian animals can be found nowhere else on earth. The Komodo dragon makes its home on the island of Komodo in eastern Indonesia. It is

This young Komodo dragon is already four feet long.

actually the world's largest monitor lizard, growing as long as ten feet (three meters) and weighing more than 300 pounds (136 kilograms). Many scientists believe that the Komodo dragon is a survivor from the days of the dinosaurs.

Herds of wild elephants roam parts of Kalimantan and Sumatra. Clouded leopards, rhinoceroses, and tigers are among the hundreds of animals that inhabit the islands of Indonesia. Tigers sometimes attack and eat people—when someone in Sumatra disappears without a trace, friends may think that a tiger ate him or her!

Orangutans swing through treetops in the Sumatran and Kalimantan jungles. *Orangutan* is an Indonesian word meaning "jungle man," given to these apes because they resemble human beings. Occasionally, Indonesian people adopt orangutans as pets. At Bukit Lawan in northern Sumatra, a rehabilitation center teaches pet orangutans how to search for food and build homes in the treetops, so that they can live in the jungle again.

A Variety of Cultures

About 350 ethnic groups live in the jungles, villages, and cities of Indonesia. Some ethnic groups number hundreds of thousands of people, while others have only a small number. Yet each has its own customs, language, and way of life. Together, all groups contribute to creating the culture of Indonesia.

The Javanese, the largest group of Indonesians, live in central and eastern Java. Most Javanese grow rice on small farms and live in whitewashed stucco houses. Some farmers' homes are next to their fields, but most live in villages and ride bicycles or walk to the fields.

The Javanese culture is very rich, dating back more than one thousand years. At one time, Java was divided into many different kingdoms, each with its own king or sultan. Two royal courts remain today, in Jogjakarta

In Bali, most artists work together as a group on a single painting.

and Solo. These palaces keep the dance, drama, and arts of the ancient Javanese culture alive.

The Balinese, who live on Bali, are well known because many tourists visit their island each year. Although most foreigners come to Bali for its beautiful, white sand beaches, the Balinese themselves tend to be afraid of the sea, where they believe evil spirits live. Instead, they consider the mountains sacred, as home to the gods of their Hindu religion. Bali has the only Hindu society outside of India.

Balinese families are usually large, with parents,

children, grandparents, aunts, and uncles living in the same house complex. Surrounded by a wall, these complexes contain several buildings—a kitchen, toilet and bath, and several bedrooms. There is usually no living or dining room, since the Balinese eat and relax outside on the porch or in the courtyard.

Perhaps nowhere else in the world does art play such an important role as in Bali. On the island, art is not considered a special talent, but is something every person can practice. Children learn to create art by becoming apprentices to the island's many stone-carvers, painters, wood-carvers, and silversmiths. Professional artists tend to live together in certain villages. For example, the painters live in Ubud, the wood-carvers in Mas, and the jewelry makers in Celuk.

Another important Indonesian group lives in the lush green mountains of western Sumatra. The Minangkabau grow rice in fields that have been carefully carved into the steep mountainsides. They use the water buffalo to help plow their fields. The buffalo plays an important role in their lives—the roofs of their houses are even shaped like buffalo horns. The houses are usually large, built of wood with tin roofs, and serve as home to more than fifty people—all related to the oldest woman in the family.

Men can have a difficult time in Minangkabau society. In the past, the Minangkabau were ruled by queens. Today, women own everything and when they die, their daughters inherit the property. In traditional Minangkabau families, the men do not even live with their wives when they marry. Instead, they stay with their mothers and just visit their wives.

The Toraja people can be found in the mountains of southern Sulawesi, one of Indonesia's most beautiful areas. They, too, are rice farmers, living in boat-shaped houses that rest on stilts among the fields. According to legend, the original Toraja arrived by sea and pulled their boats ashore, converting them into houses.

More than two hundred tribes share the jungles of Kalimantan with orangutans, gibbons, clouded leopards, and other animals. These tribes all have different customs and look different from each other. Many wear tattoos on parts of their bodies. Others practice the custom of making their ears long by putting a hole in their ear lobes and hanging heavier and heavier earrings to stretch them out. Long ear lobes are considered a sign of great beauty, but they are not as common as in the past.

Most people in the Kalimantan jungle live in longhouses which are built on stilts. Longhouses may be divided into fifty or more apartments, one for each family living there. People enter a longhouse by climbing up a log that has steps carved into it. In the past, headhunting wars were common among the tribes on

Among the people of Borneo, large earlobes are considered a sign of beauty for women.

Kalimantan, and longhouse residents pulled up the log to keep out the enemy. Today, headhunting is no longer practiced, but many longhouses are still decorated with skulls of people killed in the past.

Riches and Problems

Indonesia is rich in many natural resources. On some of the world's best farmland, plantations produce crops such as coffee, palm oil, rubber, sugarcane, tea, and tobacco. Many of these plantations were built by the Dutch, who governed the islands for almost three hundred years. Indonesia is also one of the world's largest oil producers. The nation exports more liquified natural gas than any other country, and has large reserves of tin, coal, and copper. Yet it has few manufacturing industries and imports many products.

Indonesia is a republic, governed by a president. The current president, Suharto, has led the island nation since 1968. The country's 460-member House of People's Representatives meets at least once a year in Jakarta. A larger body, the People's Consultative Assembly, meets at least once every five years to elect the president. In practice, these two bodies have little real power, though. Military officers hold several important government positions, and the president makes all important decisions.

In spite of its wealth of resources, Indonesia faces many problems. Many people are poor and must struggle to earn enough money to survive, while a smaller number are very wealthy. The population is growing very rapidly, and often there are too few jobs for the people. The government is developing programs to address these and other problems, as it attempts to build a prosperous nation. Indonesians are determined to help their country take advantage of its natural riches and play an important role as one of the world's largest nations.

2. Many Peoples, Many Cultures

Indonesians live such different lives from one another that it may be hard to believe they are citizens of the same nation. While a tribesman of the Irian highlands may prepare his bow and arrow for hunting, an engineer in Jakarta may prepare blueprints for a high-rise building on a computer, and a musician in the palace of Jogjakarta may prepare a traditional orchestra for a royal concert.

Few countries possess such a variety of cultures. Indonesia's national motto is "Unity in Diversity," which means many peoples coming together to form one country. The government has tried hard to unite the ethnic groups scattered throughout the islands.

Even so, every Indonesian identifies strongly with his or her own group. One of the first questions an Indonesian may ask a stranger is which ethnic group he or she belongs to. Not only is the culture and language of each group different, but often the members look completely different from each other. Indonesians may be the dark-skinned, curly-haired people of Irian Jaya, the lighter-skinned Javanese, or the chocolate-colored Moluccans.

In the past, Indonesians could tell which ethnic

Most Indonesians can tell which ethnic group people are from by the clothing they wear.

group a person belonged to by the way he or she dressed. Today, most people wear their traditional clothing only for festivals and weddings. On other days, the men may wear blue jeans, and the women Western-style dresses. Both men and women may also wear the traditional *sarong*, an ankle-length, wrap-around skirt decorated with a *batik* design.

Making batik cloth is one of the most well-known Javanese arts. Traditional Javanese artists create batik

Many Indonesians wear a combination of Western and traditional clothing.

by drawing or stamping a pattern on fabric with hot wax. They then dip the material in dye over and over again, until the design appears.

For special events, Indonesians put on their finest costumes. In Java, the men wear a hand-dyed sarong and a turban on their heads, folded in a certain way to show others where they come from. They also carry a sword with a wavy blade made of gold and silver, and decorated with gems. The Javanese believe that these swords will give them strength and protect them from evil. The women are also elegantly dressed in sarongs

In Irian Jaya, some men like to decorate themselves with feathers and paint on special occasions.

and *kebaya*s, lacy, tight-fitting blouses.

In Irian Jaya, the tall, dark-skinned tribesmen may spend hours painting their faces, putting bones in their noses, and decorating their bodies with feathers to prepare for festivals. The women do not decorate themselves as much as the men. They may wear shells, feathers, and skirts made of grass or rope.

Although Indonesia's groups often live differently from each other, the people share some common

characteristics. They may be friendly, sometimes start-
ing conversations with strangers as if they were old
friends. They may also try to be helpful and willing to
go out of their way for other people. In Indonesia, what
is best for the group is more important than what is
best for the individual, and people often try to make
sure that everyone is content. In village meetings, instead of accepting a majority vote, villagers will debate
the issues and make compromises until everybody is
satisfied.

A System of Cooperation

Most rural Indonesians are farmers. They live in
villages, called *kampong*s, and travel to their fields each
day on foot or by bicycle or motorcycle.

Each kampong usually includes a mosque or church
and a village meetinghouse. Larger villages may also
have a grade school, shops, and a place to hold a
market. In Indonesia, a village head, or leader, keeps
track of births, deaths, and marriages. Through meetings, the leader informs residents about government
programs and helps them plan village improvement
projects. The village may also have a music or dance
group that performs at weddings, funerals, and other
ceremonies.

In most villages, life is peaceful. The people work

hard and help each other, so that all may benefit. Indonesians follow a traditional system known as *gotong royong*, or "mutual cooperation." In this system, people cooperate to fulfill goals. When a family wants a new house, the neighbors will help build it. When an area needs a new road, the government may give the local people the materials and tell them to construct it. Even in the cities, several people may share one job, so that all can earn enough money to eat. Although Indonesia is very poor, most people do not suffer too much from poverty, since they try to share what they have.

Five Official Religions

Religion is important to Indonesians, both in their everyday life and as citizens. In Indonesia, everyone must belong to a religion, at least on paper. All Indonesians carry identity cards—similar to the way Americans carry driver's licenses. On the identify card, the person must list what religion he or she belongs to.

There are five official faiths that may be listed on the identity card. An Indonesian may be a Muslim, Hindu, Roman Catholic, Protestant, or Buddhist. Some also practice animism, which means they worship spirits in natural objects, such as trees and rivers. Although more than four out of every five Indonesians are Muslims, all religions are accepted and encouraged.

Neighborhood mosques are the site of daily worship services.

Indonesian Muslims are not as strict about some religious practices as Muslims are in the Middle East. The women do not wear veils or keep themselves hidden in their houses, as Muslim women in some other countries do. Even so, many Indonesian Muslims are deeply religious. They kneel five times a day to pray to Allah, as they call God. Like other Muslims around the world, they study the *Koran*, their religion's holy book, and do not eat pork or drink alcohol.

In Islam, Friday is the holy day. In Muslim areas of Indonesia, businesses close before 11:00 A.M. on Friday, so that people can go to the mosque, as the Muslim place of worship is called. Older Muslims may make a pilgrimage, or religious journey, to Mecca in Saudi Arabia, the holy city of Islam. So many Indonesians take this trip that special planes are chartered to take them to Jeddah, where the pilgrimage begins.

From Music to Movies

In Indonesia, music can be heard in nearly every corner of the islands. Balinese farmers returning home from the fields hear the tinkle of a traditional orchestra on the evening breeze. Nightclubs in Jakarta play American-style rock music. In homes throughout the country, people spend their free time strumming guitars and singing popular ballads. Young children may even imitate the musicians they see on television, while their friends act as the audience.

Popular Indonesian musicians often sing the folk music of their native regions. Many Indonesians say that the Batak people of northern Sumatra are the country's best musicians, but every region contributes its own special style of music. Even remote Irian Jaya has a famous rock group, known as Black Brothers.

The most common traditional music in Java and Bali is *gamelan.* The gamelan orchestra has a distinct sound created by gongs, xylophones, bronze kettles,

Gamelan *musicians perform with gongs and xylophone-like instruments.*

drums, and other instruments. The music may be played alone, or to accompany traditional dance and drama. Only men are allowed to play in a gamelan orchestra. Boys begin to learn their instruments at an early age, sitting in their fathers' laps during rehearsals.

The gamelan orchestra provides the background music for *wayang kulit*, Indonesia's traditional puppet plays, which the audience views only in shadow. Wayang kulit is performed behind a white cotton

A group of wayang kulit *puppets.*

screen, usually lit from behind by one light bulb. Those watching in front see the shadows of the flat puppets moving behind the screen. These elaborate puppets are made out of water buffalo leather. The puppet master, known as a *dalang*, controls the puppets, tells the story, and directs the gamelan players.

The stories told in the wayang kulit plays come from the Hindu religious tales which were brought to Indonesia more than a thousand years ago. Most people know the stories by heart, but still enjoy hearing them.

The shadow-puppet plays can be seen in Indonesian cities and towns, but they are most often performed in villages as part of a festival or celebration. Some performances last two or three days, continuing all night long. Children sleep on mats on the ground and wake each other up to watch their favorite parts.

Another famous art form in Java and Bali is dance. The slow-moving Javanese dances tell stories of adventure or love. Even the finger movements have meaning in these dances! Balinese folk dances are more dramatic, and the dancers dress in elaborate costumes.

On many of the other islands, movies are a popular form of entertainment. In the villages, movies are usually shown in an open-air "theater" set up in a field. Instead of the seats in an indoor theater, people bring their blankets and spread them on the ground for a place to sit. Sometimes admission is charged for these films, but at other times the government shows them for free. Vendors sell peanuts, fruit, snacks, and drinks for people to enjoy during the film.

In the cities and towns, people may watch movies made in the United States, but most villagers prefer films that are Indonesian-made. They enjoy movies about family life and romance, and are not fond of the violence found in American movies. Because scenes showing kissing or contact between the sexes are forbidden in the Muslim religion, the government cuts

Kartini is considered to be Indonesia's first feminist.

these scenes out of movies from foreign countries.

Historical movies are also popular in Indonesia. One of the most successful movies in recent years was *Kartini*, the story of a famous Indonesian heroine. Kartini was born in 1879 and lived only to the age of twenty-five. In her day, girls could not go to school but were forced to stay at home all day long. Kartini spent her short life trying to win the right to an education for girls. Her birthday is now a national holiday.

Television has only recently become common in Indonesia, and the nation's only broadcasting company is owned by the government. The government wants as many people as possible to watch television, and it has given nearly every village a television set. Even remote villages which have just had electricity for a few years now have television sets. There may be only one set in the entire village—after the people come home from the fields and say their evening prayers, they gather together to watch the nightly news. Through special programs and newscasts, the government hopes to communicate information to people all over Indonesia about topics such as health, nutrition, and family planning.

A Simple Language

The Indonesian national language is known as *Bahasa Indonesia*, which means "Indonesian language." Although all Indonesians speak the language of their own ethnic group at home or in their village, in school they learn how to speak Bahasa Indonesia. It is the language that Indonesians of different ethnic groups use to communicate with each other, and is common in the government and business.

Because it was originally developed for the use of traders, Bahasa Indonesia is a very simple language.

Traders had to be able to learn it quickly, so that they could do business. Over the years, Bahasa Indonesia absorbed words from the languages of the traders who came to the islands. Language experts have discovered words from Arabic, Portuguese, Chinese, Dutch, Spanish, and English in Bahasa Indonesia.

The Indonesian language is very poetic, with many phrases that create beautiful word pictures. For example, *mata hari*, the word for "sun," means "eye of the day." *Buah hati* means "heart's fruit," or "sweetheart," and *kamar kecil*, "the little room," is the phrase for "toilet." Indonesian is also a very logical language. The plural of many words is made by simply saying the word twice. For instance, *anak* means "child," while *anak-anak* means "children."

Indonesian names can be as simple as the language. Many Indonesians—especially those born in Java—have only one name. Even the nation's president, Suharto, has just one name.

The Indonesians have much to be proud of in their culture. They have developed a national language to communicate with people from other parts of the country. At the same time, each ethnic group maintains its own special language, culture, and customs. But most importantly, they can be proud that a people divided by more than 13,600 islands and 350 groups has come together to create a unified nation.

3. *An Ancient Heritage*

Fossils of one of the earliest ancestors of modern humans—called *homo erectus*—were first discovered in Java in 1891. Java Man, as homo erectus is also called, lived in what is now Indonesia, Asia, Africa, and Europe as many as 1.5 million years ago. This ancient human became extinct, and thousands of years passed before Indonesia's next inhabitants appeared.

The ancestors of most of today's Indonesians were Malays, a people who moved into Indonesia from the Southeast Asian mainland more than three thousand years ago. They came in waves and settled throughout the islands. Hundreds of years later, other peoples came to the islands as traders from India, China, Europe, and Arab lands. Many of them stayed, bringing ways of life that helped shape Indonesian culture and history.

Early Empires

The earliest Indonesians were sailors, following trade routes between the islands. They lived in villages, wove cloth, created ornaments to wear, and worshiped their ancestors. In many parts of the islands, this way of life remained unchanged for centuries.

A statue of Buddha sits on the upper terrace of Borobudur, the world's largest Buddhist stupa, *or shrine.*

Historians believe that Indian missionaries and traders brought the Hindu and Buddhist religions to Indonesia beginning about the fifth century A.D. Small kingdoms began to develop on Java and Sumatra, and for the next several hundred years a series of Hindu and Buddhist empires competed for power.

The Javanese and Sumatran kingdoms were ruled by kings who considered themselves gods. The Buddhist kingdom of Sailendra flourished on the plains of central Java during the eighth and ninth centuries. The people of this kingdom built Borobudur, the world's largest Buddhist shrine, which still stands today. The walls of the lowest levels of Borobudur are carved with scenes from the life of Buddha. The upper levels contain four hundred stupas—bell-shaped shrines— each with a statue of Buddha inside. A visitor to Boro- budur who wants to explore the entire monument will have to walk about 3 miles (4.8 kilometers) before reach ing the top.

The kingdom of Sailendra was defeated by the Hin- du Mataram empire during the mid-ninth and tenth centuries. The king of Mataram constructed a large Hindu temple complex—called Prambanan—just twen- ty-five miles (forty kilometers) from Borobudur.

One of the most powerful kingdoms was called Madjapahit, founded about 1292. Where earlier king- doms had ruled only parts of one island, this empire ruled Java, Bali, parts of Sumatra, and possibly other islands. About this same time, the Italian explorer Marco Polo became the first European to visit the islands, landing in Sumatra.

The Islamic religion had entered Indonesia gradu- ally over this period—Arab traders spread their Muslim faith along the trade route they followed from Europe across the Middle East and into Asia. This was the world's most important trade route at the time. Indo- nesia was an important stop because it supplied spices and valuable hardwood popular in Europe.

An artist from the Hindu kingdom of Mataram created this carving near Jogjakarta.

In the early fifteenth century, the Malaysian city of Melaka took control of the Strait of Malacca, which separates Malaysia and the Asian mainland from Sumatra and the Indonesian islands. From this position, Melaka soon controlled all trade into Asia. When the ruler of Melaka converted to Islam, the religion spread rapidly throughout the region.

Under Dutch Rule

In the sixteenth century, European traders began coming to the East Indies, as they called Indonesia, to buy the spices—especially cloves, nutmeg, and pepper—which were expensive at home. The Europeans hoped to take control of this important trade route away from the Arabs.

The Portuguese led the way, trading in the islands for nearly one hundred years. Although they set up a colony on eastern Timor Island, they had little effect on Indonesian culture as a whole. The British, too, set up trading posts in Indonesia. Like the Portuguese, they were not able to gain a more powerful position than that of merchants. The English traders were later forced to leave by the more successful Dutch.

The Dutch sent their first expedition to Indonesia in 1595, to search for openings in the islands' trade. A few years later, the Netherlands created the Dutch East

India Company by combining several private trading firms which had been competing against each other.

This new, wealthy Dutch company set up its capital at Jakarta, which it called Batavia. It soon controlled the spice trade and established a monopoly so that no other country could become involved. Although the company did not intend to be a colonial ruler, it became involved in local politics after a Javanese prince asked for help in a civil war. Over time, the Dutch gained control of more land and greater trading privileges.

The Dutch East India Company made high profits on spices and other agricultural products native to Indonesia. To increase its profits, the company began introducing new crops to the islands. The most important of these was coffee, brought from the Middle East to Java. Soon, Java's coffee came to be considered among the world's best. Even today, people may say "a cup of Java" when asking for a cup of coffee.

In 1799, the Dutch East India Company went out of business. It turned its Indonesian territory over to the Dutch government, which established a colony in the islands. The new administration set up a "culture system" that required the peasants to grow certain crops on a portion of their land. The Dutch then sold these crops in Europe to make a profit.

Although the Indonesians were paid for the coffee,

sugar, indigo, and other cash crops they grew, the prices set by the Dutch were low. Only a small fraction of each village's fields was supposed to be used to grow the crops. Soon, the crops became so profitable that the colonial government forced the people to grow more. The farmers then had less land to grow rice for food. The situation became so bad that people in parts of Java starved in the 1840s and 1850s.

The culture system made large sums of money for the Netherlands. It also led to the development of the crops that would shape Indonesia's economy for centuries— sugar, indigo, cinnamon, pepper, tea, tobacco, rubber, and palm oil. The Dutch either introduced these as new crops or grew them on a larger scale than they had been in the past.

Opposing the Dutch

Under the culture system, Indonesian peasants had to struggle to feed their families. They often lived a very difficult life. Because they were left with little energy, it is not surprising that most leaders of the anti-Dutch or nationalist movement came from the upper and educated classes.

The first revolt was begun in 1825 by a Javanese prince named Diponegoro. He was supposed to become the sultan of Jogjakarta, but the Dutch supported another prince who was more sympathetic to them. When this other prince was chosen instead of Diponegoro, he began a ten-year guerrilla war against the Dutch. Thousands died from disease, starvation, and fighting, but the people supported him. The peasants of Java were convinced that he had magical powers. He is still considered a national hero today.

As the twentieth century approached, more and more people began to oppose Dutch rule, not only in the islands but also in the Netherlands. Douwes Dekker, a former official in the Dutch Indies colonial government, wrote a book called *Max Havelaar*. For the first time, people in the Netherlands could read about the horrors Indonesians faced under colonial rule. As a result, many Dutch began to demand reforms in the colonial government.

Educated Indonesians also opposed the colonial regime. They formed educational societies which promoted national independence. The first popular nationalist group was a Muslim religious organization known as *Saraket Islam*, set up in 1911 by a group of traders.

In 1927, a young civil engineer named Sukarno founded *Partai Nasional Indonesia* to work for independence. This organization became so powerful that the Dutch made it illegal and put Sukarno in prison. But the Dutch could not stop the growing cry of *merdeka*, or freedom.

Sukarno, Indonesia's first president.

The Struggle for Independence

Although the movement for independence had begun, the Indonesians had a long struggle ahead. In 1942, the Japanese invaded and occupied the islands as part of their conquests in World War II. At first, most Indonesians were pleased that an Asian nation could overthrow the Dutch. Yet the Japanese soon proved to be even worse rulers than the Dutch.

The Japanese forced many Indonesians to work as laborers in Japan's other colonies. They jailed and tortured people they considered a threat to their power. But the Japanese did one good thing—they encouraged a sense of national pride among the Indonesians. Bahasa Indonesia was used as the everyday language, and Sukarno and other leaders were allowed to travel around the country giving patriotic speeches.

In August 1945, the Japanese surrendered to the Allied forces, leaving Indonesia without an official government. On August 17, Sukarno declared Indonesia independent. He became the first president of the Republic of Indonesia and wrote its first constitution.

Independence was short-lived because Dutch forces returned several months later. The Indonesians began a three-year battle against the Dutch, which did not end until December 1949. Thousands of Indonesians risked their lives so their country could be free.

Among those who fought for independence was an American woman known in Indonesia as *K'tut Tantri*. After seeing a documentary about Bali in a Hollywood movie theater one day in the early 1930s, this woman left on a ship bound for Jakarta. She made her way to Bali, but was not happy living the comfortable life that foreigners led in colonial Indonesia. Determined to live with the local people, she drove into the mountains one day and kept going until her car ran out of gas.

Fortunately for her, K'tut ended up in the palace of a rajah, who adopted her as his own daughter. Through the rajah's son, K'tut became involved in the Indonesian freedom movement. During World War II, she was held prisoner by the Japanese, who tortured her until she nearly died. When the Dutch returned to Indonesia, she became a radio broadcaster, spreading the news of the guerrilla war. Before Indonesia was finally free, she was forced to flee for her life and return to America. Today, K'tut is still honored by Indonesians as a revolutionary hero.

The Indonesian Nation

In 1949, the Dutch granted Indonesia its independence. Sukarno—the most famous hero of the revolution—became the new nation's first president. His speeches had stirred thousands to dedicate their lives to Indonesian independence.

Sukarno worked hard to unite the different peoples of Indonesia into one nation. At first, he was a very popular leader. He liked to think of himself as the equal to all Indonesians, and he even asked people to call him *Bung Karno*, which means "brother Karno." Yet some of his actions disturbed people. Sukarno lived a life of luxury, even though Indonesia was a poor nation. He spent large sums to build huge monuments and stadiums, while his government neglected to develop the country's industries. People soon became dissatisfied with his rule.

In 1962, Sukarno forced the Dutch government to hand over control of Irian Jaya, which it had retained after independence. He also sent troops into the newly formed state of Malaysia because he claimed some of its land should belong to Indonesia.

In 1965, the country went through a period of chaos after a political coup that tried to force a change in the government. Six generals were killed, and the Communist party was blamed. Riots broke out all over Indonesia. As many as 500,000 people were killed, many of them gunned down in the streets by angry mobs. The dead were often suspected Communists or Chinese business owners.

An unknown general named Suharto restored order. In 1968, he was elected president, a position he still holds today. Suharto was born into a peasant family and leads a simple life. He has directed the government to work on developing Indonesia's economy and social programs. One of his first successes was reducing the nation's inflation rate—the yearly increase in prices— from about 600 percent in 1966 to 9 percent by 1972.

Suharto calls his government *Pancasila* democracy. Pancasila is a philosophy that was originally created by Indonesia's first president, Sukarno. It consists of five

Suharto, Indonesia's current president, has set up many social welfare programs.

principles—belief in God, nationalism, democracy, humanitarianism (a dedication to helping all people), and justice. According to Suharto, these principles are the foundation of Indonesian government.

A Difficult Path

Since Suharto was elected, Indonesia has achieved successes in some areas. The government has built schools and hospitals, and has raised many Indonesians' standard of living. The country now produces enough rice to feed its people.

Yet the government still faces many problems. In 1975, the former Portuguese colony on eastern Timor Island became part of Indonesia, which led to fighting on and off between government troops and local guerrilla soldiers. There is also fighting in Irian Jaya, where members of the Free Papua movement are trying to gain independence for their half of the island of New Guinea.

In addition, some officials of the Indonesian government are corrupt. They steal money from the state and ask for bribes before they will help people. Indonesia's huge and growing population is another problem. Many parts of the nation are seriously overcrowded, and others are very poor.

Although Indonesia has many problems, it also has abundant and valuable natural resources. Perhaps the country's most important resource, though, is the Indonesian people. They are working hard to improve the nation and hope to create a better future for their children.

4. A Nation of Storytellers

Over the centuries, the many ethnic groups of Indonesia have created a wide variety of legends and folktales. Indonesians enjoy telling these stories over and over. Some describe the adventures of spirits, demons, and magical beings. Others offer an explanation for a fact of nature, or a tribe's customs or beginnings. Still others teach how to live a good and moral life. Many of these stories are told by only one group or on only one island, but some tales are told by parents to their children throughout Indonesia.

The Unfaithful Son

One favorite Indonesian story teaches children to love and respect their parents. The following is one version of the story of Malin Kundang.

On the coast of western Sumatra near the mouth of the Bahtang Arau River is a large gray rock. Even though it looks like an ordinary rock, people say that it was once a ship captained by a local villager named Malin Kundang.

Malin grew up in a fishing village, the only son of very poor parents who spoiled their child terribly. One day, a big ship docked nearby. Malin joined the crew, and for years no one heard anything about him. His father died, and his mother's only wish was to see her son before her life was over.

While he was away, Malin Kundang became a very successful captain. One day, a magnificent ship appeared near the village of Bahtang Arau. Although many years had passed, the villagers recognized the captain as none other than Malin Kundang.

When his mother heard the news, she was overjoyed and quickly hurried to greet her only son. Embarrassed by his poor mother, Malin ordered the crew members not to let her on the ship. "She has no son here," he said.

A short time later, Malin Kundang's ship left the village and headed for the open sea. It sailed straight into a typhoon, or huge storm, and was battered until there was almost nothing left. The ship washed ashore near the village, where it turned into a huge gray rock. Today, that rock still stands to remind people to be faithful to their parents.

The Giant's Daughter

From the island of Lombok comes this tale of Danawa Sari, the giant's daughter.

Long ago there lived a king of Lombok named

Panji Anom, who had nine wives but no children. Because he wanted children, Panji went to a sacred shrine to pray for a son who could become king after he died. When Panji had finished praying, he stopped at a stream to go fishing. Instead of a fish, he caught a box with a beautiful woman inside. Unfortunately, Panji did not know that this lady was Danawa Sari, a magical creature who was the daughter of a powerful giant. The king fell in love with her, and they were soon married.

Not long afterward, Panji's nine other wives became pregnant. Danawa Sari convinced her husband to lock them in an underground hall. After the babies were born, the giant's daughter had another evil plan. She used her magic to cut out the nine wives' eyes and send them to her father, the giant. In her hurry, she forgot to take the right eye out of one of the women.

Because eight of the wives could not see, they were unable to take care of their babies, and the children died. But the son of the one-eyed wife survived and grew strong. One day, the prince wanted to know why he was kept underground and who his father was.

After hearing the story, the prince decided to meet his father. Danawa Sari heard about the prince's plan, and she plotted another evil scheme. She decided to send the prince to her father, the giant. She told the prince that the giant would teach him magic, but secretly she planned to have the giant kill him.

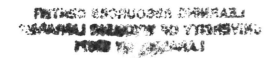

Danawa Sari wrote a letter to her father saying that the prince was a threat to her life and asking the giant to kill him. Before beginning his journey, the prince visited the king's adviser, who read the letter and rewrote it. The new letter said that the prince was the giant's grandson, and it asked the giant to teach him well and send back the eyeballs when he was finished.

The giant taught the prince all his magic. The prince learned how to fly and how to turn himself into many things, including animals and even fire. When his training was finished, the prince left for home, carrying the eyeballs.

When the prince reached the underground hall, he returned the eyes to the nine wives, who were overjoyed to be able to see again. Then he went to the palace to challenge Danawa Sari at her own magic. When she turned into a snake, so did he. When she became fire, he did the same. Finally, he defeated her, and the prince's mother became the new queen. Indonesians often tell this story to show that no matter how bad the situation may seem, there will always be justice in the end.

In the Beginning

Many Indonesian legends explain how groups of people or their customs began. The Toraja people of

The houses of Tana Toraja in South Sulawesi look like boats.

southern Sulawesi traditionally build their villages on the tops of hills. They explain this by telling the story of how their gods first stepped down from heaven onto the hilltops. They also explain the boat-shaped roofs of their houses by telling tales about how the people first came to the island by boats, which they used as houses.

Although many of the Batak people of northern Sumatra are now Christians, their traditional legends teach that the world was created from a banyan tree. Their ancient god Ampung broke one branch off the tree, and it became the fish in the lakes and streams.

Another branch turned into insects, and another into tigers and other animals. Human beings were created from the egg of a bird that had been born from another branch.

The Minangkabau people of western Sumatra tell a legend that explains the origin of their name. About six hundred years ago, they say, a king of Java tried to take over the region. Instead of going to war, the two sides decided to wage a battle between two buffalo.

The Javanese chose a huge buffalo, one of the strongest in all the land. The Minangkabau entered a baby buffalo. Unknown to the Javanese, they had put sharp razors in the baby's horns and had not fed it for three days. When the two animals were brought to the battlefield, the calf immediately rushed over to the big buffalo to suck milk from its breasts. The razors in the calf's horns split open the strong buffalo's belly, and the baby won the battle. From that day onward, the people have been known as *Minangkabau,* which means "victorious buffalo."

Sayings and Folk Beliefs

Indonesians have many sayings which they use as guides in their daily lives. People often use similar proverbs throughout the islands. One of the most popular is *Lain padang, lain belalang,* which means "In another field, another butterfly." This proverb tells people that in every place there are different customs.

If someone is impatient, a friend might tell him or her *Tak'kan lari gunung dikadjar*. In English, this means "A mountain will never run, even if you chase it." The friend is trying to tell the person to be patient and not try to force things to happen.

Indonesians often say *Buruk muka cermin dibelah*, which means "Do not break the mirror if your face is ugly." If someone says this to you, they are saying you should not blame others for your own faults.

Few people in the world follow more folk beliefs than the Indonesians. Because most Indonesians live in the country, many folk beliefs involve animals. In Sulawesi, the Toraja people believe that if they see a snake while they are traveling, they should turn around and head home. A snake is bad luck. If a cat crosses their path, though, it brings good luck.

Many Javanese people believe that if a butterfly flies into the house, guests will arrive soon. They may also think that a dream about losing a tooth means that a family member will die soon.

Some tribes in Kalimantan will not leave to go hunting unless a bird flies in front of them from right to left on the day that they plan to depart. In the Maluku islands, three is an unlucky number. The people who live there believe that three people should never appear in a photograph together. If this happens, one of them will have trouble—perhaps he or she will be separated from the other two, or even die.

Today, many people—especially in the cities—no longer follow these folk beliefs. Like Indonesia's folktales and legends, though, they contribute to the colorful culture of the islands.

5. The Festival Islands

With its hundreds of different ethnic groups, Indonesia is a land with a wide variety of festivals and ceremonies. It may seem as if someone is always celebrating, somewhere on the islands! Indonesian groups honor every occasion in life, from birth to death. Each group has its own special celebrations—some may throw a buffalo into the crater of a smoking volcano, while others may honor the birds of the jungle. Several holidays are observed by the majority of Indonesians.

Hari Raya

Since most Indonesians are Muslims, Hari Raya is the country's most important holiday. Hari Raya celebrates the end of Ramadan, the Muslim month of fasting. Because the Muslim calendar follows the cycles of the moon, its months are shorter than those of the Western calendar, and Hari Raya falls at a different date each year.

During the month of Ramadan, Muslims are not allowed to eat or drink from sunrise to sunset. Indonesian Muslims rise early in the morning to pray and have breakfast, and then must wait until sundown to

Balinese girls perform their traditional dances from a very young age.

eat dinner. People may find it difficult to work during Ramadan, because they are hungry and thirsty. To honor their accomplishment, at the end of Ramadan they celebrate Hari Raya, a two-day holiday feast.

People may stay up all night before Hari Raya to prepare food for the feast. About 7:00 A.M., Hari Raya begins as Muslims go to the mosque to pray. They dress in their finest sarongs and gold jewelry, and spend the next two days visiting friends. At each house, people eat cakes, cookies, and a spicy Indonesian dish known as curry. It is important not to eat too much at each house, or a serious stomachache could be the result!

Another holiday celebrated throughout Indonesia is Independence Day on August 17. It marks the anniversary of the day Indonesia became independent from the Dutch in 1945. Each area celebrates Independence Day in its own way. In Jakarta and other cities, people watch parades, listen to speeches, and attend sporting events and cultural performances. In Irian Jaya, tribes perform the dances they once performed after victory in battle. In the Riau Islands on the northwestern edge of Indonesia, people celebrate with boat races and a twenty-eight-mile (forty-five-kilometer) walkathon.

Cockfighting

One important part of most Indonesian festivals is

Two roosters prepare for a cockfight in Bali.

cockfighting. It is difficult for people outside of Indonesia to understand the importance these fights play in
the lives of Indonesian men. For many men, a fighting
cock is their most valuable possession. In Balinese villages, cockfighting roosters hang in cages outside of
nearly every house. The Balinese display the birds
proudly, and they believe the birds are entertained by the
people passing by.

A cockfight is usually finished in a matter of

seconds. Each bird has a razor tied to one leg. As soon as the two roosters are released into the ring, they attack each other in a flurry of feathers. One of them is soon sliced with the razor. The dead rooster goes home to be cooked for dinner, and the winner will enter other fights.

Indonesian men are as enthusiastic about cockfighting as many Americans are about baseball or football. During a village cockfight, as many as one hundred men may stand around the ring, watching and placing bets. Women are rarely seen at the fights.

Betting on the cocks is fast-paced, and a fortune may be won or lost in a single afternoon. In 1986, the Indonesian government outlawed gambling, including cockfighting, to prevent people from losing their money. Now, Indonesians must get permission from the local authorities to hold a cockfight. This law has not stamped out cockfighting, however, because it is easy to get permission if a cockfight is part of a ceremony. There are so many ceremonies in Indonesia that cockfights are as popular as ever.

The Festival Island

Few places in Indonesia have more festivals than Bali. The Balinese spend much of their time preparing for ceremonies and celebrations—hardly a week goes by when there is not a festival somewhere on the island. Although they usually take place at a temple, Balinese festivals are also social occasions, with much eating, drinking, and cockfighting.

The biggest Balinese celebration, Galungan, takes place every 210 days. During this three-day holiday, Bali's Hindus worship their supreme god, Sanghyang Widi. The Balinese believe that the spirits of their ancestors return to earth for this festival. On the first day, people prepare food and offerings, on the second they pray at the temple, and on the third they visit friends. It is one of the busiest times of the year, and it may seem as if everyone in Bali is out on the roads during Galungan.

The Balinese have ceremonies to mark most events in a person's life. The tooth filing ceremony happens when boys and girls are between fifteen and seventeen years of age. It shows that the teenager has become an adult. The young person's teeth are filed as a sign that evil has been filed away. In the past, the teeth were filed until they were perfectly even, but today they are only lightly touched.

On the day of the ceremony, the women of the family rise before dawn to prepare food for the guests and elaborate offerings of fruit and flowers for the gods. A religious leader directs the ceremony, and a special tooth filer files the young person's front teeth.

A Balinese priest blesses villagers as part of a Hindu temple ceremony.

After the ceremony is finished, family and friends gather for a feast.

In Bali, funerals are not sad but happy occasions, when the spirit of the dead person is released from the body to be born again in the body of another person. Hindus believe that if someone is good during his or her lifetime, the next life will be better; if someone is bad, it will be worse.

The body of the dead person is carried high on a wooden tower in the middle of a procession of musicians, family members, and friends. The tower is tossed about so the soul cannot find its way home to bother the living relatives. The sound of the gongs, gamelan, and gossip create a happy atmosphere as the participants wait for the tower to be set on fire. They believe that burning the body will free the dead person's spirit. After the tower is lit, the celebration continues.

Torajan Feast of the Dead

Another Indonesian group that holds elaborate funerals is the Toraja in the highlands of southern Sulawesi. When a Torajan dies, it can take weeks, months, or even years to prepare for the funeral and gather all the family members together. The funeral will last three, five, or seven nights, since an odd number is considered lucky.

A large group of family members makes its way to the cre-mation ground for a Balinese funeral.

Some Torajan funerals can cost thousands of dollars and put the family into debt for generations. As many as one hundred buffalo may be slaughtered to feed the many guests who come from all over Indonesia. The family builds a village of temporary houses for the visitors to stay in. After the funeral, the family may either tear these buildings down or save them for a future ceremony.

The Toraja people bury the bodies of their dead in caves high up the sides of cliffs. In front of each cave is a platform holding *tau tau*, wooden figures carved to look like the people inside. During the funeral, family members and friends wail and moan, yet at the same time guests feast and enjoy themselves. Dancers and singers provide entertainment, and men participate in sports competitions.

Centuries-Old Customs

Many Indonesian celebrations have not changed much in hundreds of years. On the small island of Sumba, a ritual battle takes place every April. Men on horseback fight each other with spears until one person is killed. This tradition dates from the days when the tribe sacrificed human beings. The women watch the battle nervously, praying that their husbands and sons will survive unharmed.

One of the most famous events in Indonesia is the annual bull races on the island of Madura. Trial races are held over several months to choose the fastest bulls in each region of Madura. The finals take place in the capital, Pemekasan. On the morning of the Grand Final Race, the forty-eight competing bulls parade through the streets of the city. When race time draws near, the gamelan orchestras begin to play. The bulls are paired into teams of two, each with a jockey riding on a wooden stand between them. The winning pair becomes famous on the island.

Although few Buddhists remain in Indonesia, every year on Buddha's birthday the Kassada Festival takes place at Mount Bromo in eastern Java. The Tenggerese people who live around this live volcano practice a religion that mixes beliefs from Hinduism and Buddhism. On festival day, the villagers climb to the top of the smoking crater, and throw cows and chickens into the fire below. They believe that sacrificing animals will make the volcano remain inactive. It must work, since the last eruption occurred more than fifty years ago!

The Iban—one of the main tribes in Kalimantan—celebrate Hornbill Feast once a year in honor of the big-beaked birds that fly through the jungle treetops. During the festival, each family in a longhouse displays its valuable possessions, and the women and girls wear their finest jewelry. Pigs are slaughtered because the Iban believe that the spirits of the dead pigs will carry messages to their ancestors in the next world. The pigs' livers are examined as a form of fortune-telling to see if the family will have luck in the days ahead.

Family members parade huge hornbill sculptures up and down the balcony of the longhouse and then place them on tall poles. From there, the hornbills stand guard over the festival. The fasting lasts for three days. People eat special dishes of rice, vegetables, pig, and fish, and drink *tuak*, a wine made from the sap of the palm tree.

The Balinese, Torajan, and Iban festivals are just a few of the many celebrations that take place on Indonesia's islands. Hundreds of holidays are observed by the country's ethnic groups. Throughout Indonesia, people gather together to celebrate the important events in their lives, to honor their gods, and to give thanks for all they have received.

6. *Family Life and Spicy Food*

Life in Indonesia centers on villages or neighborhoods. Although people in the country live differently from those in the city, their values are similar. Relationships with family and friends are usually considered more important than earning a lot of money or having a lot of possessions.

Life in Indonesian villages follows traditional patterns. Rural families rise at the break of dawn. If they are Muslim, they say their first prayers of the day. After eating a breakfast of rice with vegetables or salted fish, the parents leave for the rice fields, and the children start walking to school.

After school, children usually help with the chores, such as cleaning the house or tending the garden. Older children frequently take care of their younger brothers or sisters. In the evening, they do their homework by the light of a kerosene lamp if there is no electricity, and bathe in a river or from a big barrel of water called a *mandi.* Even in the cities, the bath is a large, tiled water tank. Bathers dip out water with a plastic pan, pour it over themselves, soap up, and rinse off with another pan of water. The water is cold, but it feels good after a hot Indonesian day. After taking a bath, rural children

A woman and her daughters work together in a village in central Java.

may go with their parents to visit friends or take a walk around the village to talk to neighbors.

Life in the City

Even though most rural Indonesians feel strong ties to the villages where they live, every year some leave to go to Jakarta and other cities in search of a job and a higher standard of living. Yet few high-paying jobs are available, and newcomers often must live in huts made of paper and tin in crowded slums. To earn a living,

Becaks *serve as bicycle taxis in Indonesian cities and towns.*

many men drive *becaks*, the three-wheeled bicycle taxis found in towns and cities throughout Indonesia. Women often find work as servants in the homes of middle- and upper-class Indonesians.

Although poor Indonesians must usually struggle to survive, life is easier for those in the middle and upper class. They, too, rise as early as 5:00 A.M., since work and school often begin at 7:00 A.M. After a breakfast of fried rice with a fried egg on the side, the children either walk to school or wait for the school bus, and their fathers leave for work. Some middle- and upper-class Indonesian women have careers, but most stay home to take care of the house and children, and become involved in social clubs and associations.

Children are often home from school by early afternoon, when they eat lunch. Lunch may be fried rice or noodles, chicken, fish, or another dish eaten with a plate of rice and vegetables, or fried tempe, an inexpensive high-protein food made from soybeans. Poorer Indonesians often eat tempe or bean curd rather than meat. After lunch, children do their homework and rest in the heat of the day.

Since well-to-do families have servants to do most of the housekeeping, the families have free time to enjoy themselves in the evenings. They begin with dinner, which is similar to lunch but usually includes more dishes. Family members have a plate of rice in front of them and can serve whatever else they wish to eat from large dishes at the center of the table. Often, one of these will be a soup to spoon over the rice and give it more flavor. Another will be *sambal*, or chili paste. Diners mix sambal with the rice and other dishes to make them more spicy.

After dinner, families may go to a movie, to the mosque to pray, or to the night market. Here, stalls sell household goods and clothes, and vendors prepare delicious meals and snacks. Families may also go to visit friends. Indonesians often stop at a friend's house

A house in a wealthy Jakarta neighborhood.

without telephoning first. When guests arrive, the host encourages them to sit in the living room and gives them tea, cakes, and cookies. If it is dinnertime, they will be invited to stay for a meal.

Spicy Foods

Indonesian cooking is a blend of spices and flavors reflecting the many foreign peoples that lived in the islands over the centuries. Curry, a dish of meat or vegetables in a spicy sauce served over rice, came from India. Fried rice and noodles were brought by the Chinese. The *rijstafel*, or rice table, a buffet feast with many dishes, was created by the Dutch.

Each region of Indonesia has its own style of cooking. The Javanese use a lot of sugar, so their food is very sweet. The Minangkabau prefer their dishes as spicy as possible. Some Indonesians even eat foods that would not be eaten by other Indonesians. The Balinese, for example, eat many dishes made with pork. These dishes could not be eaten by Indonesian Muslims, since eating pork is forbidden by their religion.

In spite of these differences, some foods are eaten throughout Indonesia. These include *sate*, skewers of barbecued meat. Sate can be made from chicken, beef, or pork, but goat is the most popular. Before eating, diners dip the sate in a spicy peanut sauce.

Gado gado can be found in most places in Indonesia. A nutritious salad, gado gado is a mixture of vegetables such as potatoes, cabbage, and bean sprouts, covered with a spicy peanut sauce. It is eaten with crunchy shrimp crackers known as *krupuk*, which are a favorite Indonesian snack.

Most people in Indonesia eat rice with every meal. In the highlands of Sumatra, though, people prefer corn, and in Irian Jaya, sweet potatoes are the main food. In the eastern islands, sago—a kind of sticky bread—forms a part of the diet. Sago flour is made by cutting a sago palm tree in half lengthwise and pounding it for many hours. Although sago is the main part of many Indonesians' diets, it is low in protein and not particularly nutritious.

Poor nutrition remains a major problem in many villages—thousands of children become sick because they do not have the right foods to eat. Some families cannot afford to buy healthful food, and many people do not know which foods they should eat to be healthy. The government is attempting to educate mothers about good nutrition, but it is a slow process.

To Market, to Market

In Indonesia there are many ways to buy food and everyday items. Although many people in the cities shop

Many Indonesian peddlers set up shop on sidewalks.

in modern supermarkets, most Indonesians still buy groceries at the *pasar*, or traditional market. In the country, the market is often held on a street or other open area, but in the city it may be inside a building.

In smaller villages, the market takes place only once a week, but in towns and cities it is usually open every day. Within the market are stalls selling meat, fruit, and vegetables. The prices are not marked, and people bargain with the vendor for the best price.

Shoppers usually ask for a lower price than what the vendor wants, and the two argue until they reach a compromise.

Indonesians in the towns and cities can shop in another, more convenient way. Many of the items they need to buy are brought to the gates in front of their homes. From morning until evening, peddlers walk up and down the streets selling items that range from medicine to meat. Trucks loaded with furniture may drive by, in case people want to buy a new chair or couch.

In the evening, the "walking restaurants" make their rounds of the neighborhoods. These vendors sell food from their carts, and each cook has his own specialty. Each cart is a full kitchen, with a charcoal grill for sate, or a burner and frying pan for cooking fried noodles or other specialties. Often, the food these vendors prepare is so popular that it is sold out long before the evening is over.

Indonesians may also choose to go out to eat. One very popular type of restaurant is a *nasi Padang* ("Padang rice") restaurant. Named after the west Sumatran city of Padang, these restaurants serve spicy Minangkabau food. Other Indonesians choose to eat at a *warung*, or roadside stall. A warung usually sells only one dish, but since the cook specializes in that dish, it can be some of the best food available in Indonesia.

One favorite warung food is *soto ayam*, or chicken

A neighborhood vendor grills sate in the front yard of a Jakarta home.

soup. It is served with lime and a huge plate of rice, making it a full meal. Some warung sell only soft drinks, tea, and coffee. Others specialize in desserts such as *es campur*, which means "ice mix." It is a dish of shaved ice topped with coconut, cubes of gelatin dessert, pineapple and other fruit, and a sweet sauce.

Tropical Fruit

In Indonesia, fruit is plentiful, cheap, nutritious, and delicious. Indonesians enjoy eating fruit. People in

Although it has a horrible odor, the sweet, creamy durian fruit is eaten by nearly all Indonesians.

rural areas pick it straight from the tree, while those in towns and cities buy fruit at the market.

Perhaps the most unusual Indonesian fruit is the *durian*. This large, green, spiky fruit has a creamy white interior and an unpleasant smell—similiar to an open sewer! In spite of its smell, the fruit is delicious and is a favorite in most Southeast Asian countries. The smell of the ripe durian is so unpleasant, though, that the fruit is sometimes not allowed on airplanes or in hotels.

A tasty Indonesian fruit is the *mangosteen*, which has a hard, thick, purple shell and sweet, white segments inside. Another Indonesian fruit—the *salak*—is sometimes called the "snake fruit" because its brown peel resembles a snake skin. Inside, though, are whitish, crunchy, slightly sour sections.

The huge jackfruit can weigh more than forty pounds (eighteen kilograms). On the outside, it is green and spiky like a durian, but the inside is full of sweet, yellow pieces of fruit. The Indonesians eat jackfruit as a fruit when it is ripe and sweet, but they also pick it before it is ripe and cook it with coconut milk as a vegetable dish.

More than fifteen varieties of bananas can be found throughout Indonesia. These range from tiny, sweet fruit to huge bananas with big, black seeds. Coconut palms also grow in most parts of the islands. Indonesians use coconut milk in curries, meat and vegetable dishes, and in a drink called *es kelapa muda*, or "iced young coconut." To make this drink, they cut open an unripe coconut, pour the juice into a glass, and scrape the slippery white fruit from the inside of the shell, adding it to the glass along with ice. Es kelapa muda is a refreshing drink on a hot Indonesian day.

Cooking Indonesian

It is difficult to cook Indonesian food in the United States because so many of the ingredients are not available in American stores. Even if they are, many dishes are time-consuming to prepare. These recipes are for three of Indonesia's most popular dishes. They can be made from ingredients available at almost any super-market. You may wish to ask an adult to help you prepare these dishes.

Nasi Goreng (Fried Rice)

2 cups uncooked rice (preferably not instant rice)
5 shallots or 1/2 onion
3 cloves garlic
4 tablespoons oil
1/2 pound shrimp (frozen shrimp is the easiest to use)
3 tablespoons soy sauce
1 thinly sliced hot red pepper (optional)
1 cucumber

Cook the rice according to the directions on the package. While the rice is cooking, chop the shal-lots (or onion) finely and mince the garlic. Place the shallots, garlic, and oil in a skillet and fry them until the shallots are soft. (Although you can use a skillet, a wok works better, if you have one.) Add the shrimp, and cook a few minutes longer. Add the soy sauce and hot red pepper (if desired), and stir. Then add the rice, and mix thoroughly. Spoon the mixture onto a large serving platter. Slice the cucumber and place it on the side of the platter. This should serve four people.

Sate

2 shallots or 4 green onions
1 teaspoon ground coriander
2 cloves garlic
2 teaspoons lemon juice
3 tablespoons soy sauce
1-1/2 tablespoons brown sugar
1 pound beef steak cut into thin, one-inch slices
wooden skewers
1 cucumber

Slice the shallots very thin, and place them in a small bowl together with the coriander, garlic, lemon juice, soy sauce, and brown sugar. Add the meat, and mix thoroughly. Let the mixture sit in the refrigerator for at least two hours, but preferably overnight. After the meat has absorbed the spices, it can be cooked. Put four or five pieces of meat on each skewer and either barbecue it on a barbecue pit or broil it in the oven. Cooking the meat in a broiler takes about three minutes on each side. Place the cooked meat on a serving platter. Slice the cucumber and serve it with sate.

Sate should be dipped in peanut sauce before it is eaten. A recipe for peanut sauce follows.

Sate Peanut Sauce

2 tablespoons peanut butter
1 teaspoon soy sauce
3 teaspoons lemon juice
6 tablespoons water
1 shallot (or 1 green onion)
pinch of cayenne pepper

In a small bowl, mix the peanut butter, soy sauce, lemon juice, and water thoroughly. Slice the shallot very thinly. Add the shallot and the cayenne pepper to the sauce. Serve it with the sate.

For dessert, you may want to try es campur. This popular dessert can be made in a variety of ways, and every region of Indonesia has its own style. Because the kinds of fruit and the amount of ingredients can vary, you are encouraged to be creative in preparing this Indonesian treat!

Es Campur

Basic Ingredients
5 or more ice cubes per person
grenadine or sno-cone syrup
sweetened condensed milk (optional)

Toppings (Choose your favorites)
pineapple pieces (canned pineapple rings cut into small pieces)
small cubes of gelatin dessert (any flavor)
a few tablespoons of canned corn
a few tablespoons of canned kidney beans
young coconut cut into small pieces (may be bought in a can)
chopped mandarin orange segments (canned) or pieces of fresh orange

Crush the ice cubes in a blender and place them in a small bowl. Use a separate bowl for each person you are serving. (If you have an ice shaver, shaved ice is more authentic, but crushed ice is also fine.) Place your choice of toppings—fruit pieces, gelatin dessert, corn, and beans—on top of the ice. Pour the grenadine or sno-cone syrup (and the sweetened condensed milk, if you desire) over the top of the ingredients. Use a spoon to enjoy this tasty dessert!

7. *School Days*

When Indonesia was a Dutch colony, few Indonesians received an education. Only the people who were being trained for positions in Dutch businesses or government were allowed to attend school. By the time the country became independent, only a few hundred Indonesians had graduated from high school, and there was only one university in the entire nation.

The situation is different today. The government has built many schools, colleges, and teacher-training institutes. All Indonesian children are required to attend school from age six to twelve. Today, more than two out of every three Indonesians can read and write.

It can be difficult for some parents to send their children to school because education in Indonesia is not free. For each student, parents must pay a small fee and purchase their textbooks and three different uniforms. The government will help parents who cannot afford the fee, though, and most parents try hard to send their children to school.

Even so, many Indonesian children must drop out of school—some after only a few years of education— to work to help their families survive. Rural parents may need help in the rice fields, and city children may have to sell newspapers, candy, or cigarettes on the streets to help support their families.

The School System

Indonesia's educational system is similar to the American system, with a six-year grade school, three-year junior high, and three-year high school. About 90 percent of all children complete grade school. Although it is not required, increasing numbers enter junior high and high school every year.

The public schools—known as government schools in Indonesia—do not have kindergartens. Some parents choose to send their children to private two-year kindergartens, which charge tuition. Here, they learn how to play with other children, draw, count, and recite the alphabet.

Most children begin *sekolah dasar*, or grade school, at age six. Although the majority attend government schools, some students choose private or Christian schools because their parents feel the education there is better. Muslim parents sometimes send their children to *madrasah*, or Muslim schools, which emphasize the teachings of Islam.

Grade-school students in Indonesia spend less time in the classroom than American students. In the first and second grades, they go to school for only about

Students at Sekolah Dasar Latihan in Jakarta talk together during recess.

three hours each day. Even so, the children are expected to do several hours of homework every evening.

Beginning with grade three, the school day becomes longer, usually five hours. Third-grade students study a larger number of subjects and join the *pramuka*, or scouts. In most countries, scouting is an after-school activity which children may choose to participate in. In Indonesia, every child joins the scouts—it is scheduled as a regular class, with boys and girls together in the same group. Like Boy Scouts and Girl Scouts in the United States, Indonesian pramuka members learn camping skills, knot tying, and ways to survive in the wilderness.

In Indonesia, all students study religion in school. The subject of *agama*, or religion, is not a class about different religions—instead, students receive religious training about their own faith, taught by a teacher from their faith. Muslim students learn how to pray, and how to follow the laws of Islam. Beginning in the third grade, they are also taught to read and write Arabic, the language of the Koran. Christian students attend a separate class, where they may study the Bible.

In another class, students study the five principles of Pancasila. These principles—belief in God, nationalism, democracy, humanitarianism, and justice—are ones the Indonesian government tries to follow. The class is called P.M.P., which stands for *Perdidikan* (education), Morality, and Pancasila. In this course, the students study the meaning of the five Pancasila principles and learn how they can contribute to Indonesian society by being good citizens. P.M.P. is one of the most important subjects studied every year. If students do not pass it, they cannot advance to the next grade.

A Jakarta School

A visit to the fifth-grade class of Sekolah Dasar Latihan, a public school in Jakarta, gives an idea of what life is like for students in Indonesia. Although some schools have classes in the afternoon, S.D. Latihan—like most others—is a morning school. Indonesian students prefer to go to school in the morning, before the heat of the midday sun makes it difficult to study in classrooms that are not air-conditioned. In most grade schools, one *guru*, or teacher, teaches all subjects except sports and religion, but in S.D. Latihan, a different person teaches each subject.

On Monday, the six-day school week begins with a special ceremony known as *upacara*. The students arrive before 7:00 A.M., neatly dressed in the school uniform—a white blouse and red skirt for girls, and a white shirt and red pants for boys. The children line up outside the school building in rows facing the flagpole.

An honor patrol of three students marches to the flagpole and raises the flag while everyone sings *Indonesia Raya*, the national anthem. All students bow their heads to pray for the national heroes of Indonesia. The principal then makes a series of announcements, and the students recite the five principles of Pancasila. After upacara closes with the singing of another national song, the children march into their classrooms.

For the fifth grade, the school week begins with religion class. On this particular day, the class is for Muslims. Christian students go to the library to read, since their class is on Saturday.

A fifth-grade class studies Bahasa Indonesia, the national language.

On this Monday, the fifth graders also participate in sports, usually soccer or other games. The last subject of the day is the Indonesian language. In this class, the teacher begins by reading a folktale or story about one of the country's national heroes. She asks the students to repeat what they have heard in their own words, and quizzes them on vocabulary that appears in the story. The students then close their books and wait to be dismissed at noon, when the school day is over.

In an Indonesian grade school, the students study only a few subjects each day, and every day the subjects are different. On other days at S.D. Latihan, the children might attend classes in mathematics, history, social studies, P.M.P., crafts, music and dancing, and scouts—for a total of fifteen subjects. There are three or four classes per day, with two ten-minute recesses. During this time, the children can talk to their friends or buy soft drinks and food at a snack bar.

Village Schools

Students in rural areas of Indonesia live a different life-style than those in the city, but the schools they attend are not that different from S.D. Latihan. Government schools follow the same curriculum and use the same books throughout the country. Village students also join the scouting movement.

Although the Indonesian government has built many schools, some smaller villages still do not have a school building. Children in these villages can attend classes in another village if they wish. They may have to walk a mile or more through rice fields to get to school, but many are willing to do so in order to obtain an education.

Most village children drop out of school after the sixth grade. Often, their parents cannot afford to send them to junior high school, which is usually located in a larger town. Instead, they are needed at home to help in the fields. Those who wish to continue their education may commute by bus or live with relatives in a larger town so they can go to school.

Junior High and Beyond

Although many Indonesian students drop out of school after the sixth grade, about 30 percent go on to attend junior high, known in Indonesian as *sekolah menengah pertama*. Here, they study the same subjects as in grade school, but on a more advanced level. When they reach high school, though, they may face some difficult choices.

In Indonesia, there are several different types of high schools. Students who wish to enter a university may attend a high school where they take special courses to prepare for college. Students who would like to receive practical training to become a machinist, mechanic, or architect can enter a technical high school. Two other kinds of Indonesian high schools train teachers. The first prepares students to teach grade school, while the second trains high schoolers to be gym teachers in elementary schools. In order to enter any Indonesian high school, students must pass a difficult examination.

Most students who complete the college preparation courses take the entrance examination for one of

These high school students practice jumping hurdles as they prepare to be gym teachers.

the government universities. During this test, students are quizzed on everything they have learned during their previous years of schooling. The test is so difficult that only about 20 percent of those who take it pass. Those who fail may take it again the following year or may enroll in a private university. Private universities are expensive, though, costing almost ten times more than government schools. Of the forty-nine government universities and educational institutes, the largest is the University of Indonesia in Jakarta, with more than ten thousand students.

Because only a small percentage of all Indonesians attend a university, those who do may feel that it is a privilege, and they study hard. Although the schools offer many majors, the most popular are engineering, medicine, and business—especially for male students. Women tend to study the arts, literature, and foreign languages. Women make up about half of the university students in Indonesia, although on some campuses they form a majority.

Because Indonesian colleges and universities do not provide dormitories, students must find a place to live on their own. Some stay with their families or relatives. Others live in private boarding houses, where they pay for a room and meals, or maybe just a room. If no meals are served, the students may get together as a group and hire a servant to cook for them.

Successes and Failures

The government of Indonesia has made education a priority, and it spends a great deal of money on building new schools. Yet there are still many problems with the overall quality of Indonesian education.

Finding good teachers ranks as a major problem. Teachers' salaries are very low and not enough people enter the field. It is especially difficult to get teachers to work in remote areas, where they will be far from friends and relatives. The government pays higher salaries to teachers willing to work in Kalimantan, Sulawesi, Irian Jaya, and the outer islands, but there are not enough teachers to meet the needs of the population.

Low salaries are also a problem in the universities. Professors are paid so little that they must sometimes hold three or four jobs to support their families. They often turn their classes over to assistants rather than teaching themselves.

Indonesia has improved its educational system dramatically since it became independent. In spite of the many difficulties in educating its huge, spread-out population, the government continues to work to better the education of all Indonesians. The people believe that by educating its citizens, Indonesia can progress toward a better future.

8. Sports for Fun

October 1, 1988, was a special day in the history of Indonesia. On this day, the women's archery team won the country's first Olympic medal, at the summer Olympic games in Seoul, Korea. Throughout Indonesia, people celebrated this day of national pride.

Although few Indonesians can afford the expensive equipment needed for archery, people across the country enjoy many sports, particularly team sports such as badminton, soccer, volleyball, and basketball. Children participate in sports both in school and after school for fun. Most adults, though, enjoy watching sports rather than participating.

Badminton is one of the country's favorite sports. Similar to tennis, it can be played with two individuals (called singles), or with two teams of two people each (called doubles). Players hit a nylon shuttlecock, or birdie, back and forth across a net without letting it touch the ground. The winner is the first person to score fifteen points in a men's game, or eleven points in a women's game.

Indonesia has produced a number of world badminton champions. Rudy Hartono won badminton's All-England Informal World Championship seven years in

Badminton is a popular sport, and Indonesian teams have competed in international matches.

a row. Indonesian players have also won the Thomas Cup men's division championship and the Uber Cup women's championship many times. The top badminton players are considered national heroes. During matches, the whole country waits eagerly for the results.

Although Indonesians like to watch professional players, they also enjoy playing badminton themselves. Even in the most remote villages, children who cannot afford to buy proper badminton equipment may use their rubber slippers as rackets and set up a clothesline for the net.

Soccer's Popularity Soars

Although badminton has many fans, no sport is more popular in Indonesia than soccer. It is so popular that the country has built the world's largest indoor soccer stadium, with room for one hundred thousand fans.

As with badminton, poor children are not discouraged when they lack the proper equipment for soccer. They may use homemade soccer balls, piles of clothes or shoes in place of goalposts, or play on dirt fields in their bare feet. Some children become excellent players in these informal games, and they may be asked to play on amateur soccer teams sponsored by corporations. These teams play each other at stadiums around the country. The best players join the regional teams, and the best of these may become members of the national amateur team.

Corporations also sponsor professional soccer teams in Indonesia. So many corporations want to sponsor teams that some cities have more than one—Jakarta has about ten! Professional soccer is organized differently in Indonesia than in the United States. The players are not paid to be full-time athletes but are hired as employees of the corporation and play soccer in their spare time.

Many children also play volleyball and basketball, both as school sports and for fun. Badminton, soccer,

Village boys play soccer.

volleyball, and basketball are part of *Karang Teruna*, an organization sponsored by the Indonesian government for young people between the ages of ten and twenty-five. The members of Karang Teruna play sports and enjoy social activities organized by a neighborhood leader.

In recent years, running has become popular in the islands. Because Indonesia has such hot weather, people must go jogging very early in the morning. On the streets of Jakarta and other cities at 6:00 A.M., many people are out on a morning jog. For the past several years, Indonesia has sponsored the Bali 10K Paradise Run. This race has attracted top runners from around the world.

Traditional Sports

Before Western sports such as soccer and badminton were introduced to Indonesia, the people played games that had developed on the islands. Although these Indonesian sports were traditionally for boys, today both boys and girls practice them.

One traditional Indonesian sport is *pencak silat*, a type of martial art that is sometimes called *silat*. Pencak silat is not just a form of self-defense, though. Like other Asian martial arts, its discipline helps develop the minds and spirits of those who practice it.

Each area of Indonesia has created its own style of silat. In the palace of Jogjakarta, a *keris*—a type of dagger with a wavy blade—is used. West Sumatra's Minangkabau-style silat is like a dance with self-defense movements. In western Java, silat performers stand still but move their hands very quickly. In eastern Java, people performing pencak silat carry a sickle-shaped sword. In southern Sulawesi, they use a small knife.

Although many types of pencak silat have become more like dances and are performed at celebrations, other types are still learned for self-defense. Since the goal of silat is to use the opponent's energy against him or her, those who practice it do not have to be big or strong. In silat competitions, participants score points for punches, kicks, and tripping the opponent during three-minute rounds.

There are more than eight hundred pencak silat clubs in Indonesia. Although most are sports clubs that anyone can join, a few pencak silat groups are more like secret societies—only carefully chosen people are invited to be members. These groups often meet at midnight and may practice secret rituals.

Another traditional team sport played in Sumatra and other places is *sepak takraw*. Similar to volleyball, takraw is played on a court where players must keep a ball moving back and forth over a net. But there the

Boys and girls in Solo prepare for a demonstration of pencak silat.

similarity ends. In takraw, players can use only their heads, legs, and feet to move the ball. The ball is smaller than that used in volleyball and is made of woven rattan.

Indonesians also enjoy kite flying. Many people fly pretty kites just for fun, but some compete in kite-flying contests. In these, players rub glass dust on the strings of their kites. After the kites are in the air, the players try to break the strings of the other kites by rubbing the glass dust against them. The winner is the person whose kite string remains unbroken. Indonesian kites do not look like the diamond-shaped ones flown in the United States. Instead, they have a special design using an oval and a crescent, with fringes hanging from the corners.

Some Indonesian ethnic groups have created their own sports. In western Java, the Sundanese people practice *benjang*, a form of wrestling using foot-long sticks. The opponents hit each other's legs with the sticks until one of them is knocked down. In southern Sulawesi, the Toraja men play *sisemba*, a type of kick-boxing. Sisemba can be played with just two people or an entire village. The teams fight each other until one team has been kicked to the ground.

The people of the Riau Islands play a game known as *gasing*, or wooden tops. Players use tops that are about the size of a baseball. One person spins his top in the center of a circle that has been drawn on the ground. The other player throws his top at the first one, trying to stop it. The winner is the owner of the top that continues to spin the longest.

From unusual games such as kick-boxing to those known around the world, sports form an important part of Indonesian life. The Indonesian people play sports enthusiastically and enjoy watching them as well. Although most people cannot afford expensive equipment, they invent many ways to play sports and have fun.

9. *Beginning in a New Land*

Many people from other lands have come to Indonesia over the centuries, creating a country that is a blend of many cultures. Yet the Indonesians themselves have been unwilling to leave their homes. They feel strong ties to their families, friends, villages, and culture—even to the land they farm. The word that Indonesians use to distinguish themselves from the Chinese, Dutch, Arabs, and other peoples who have lived in the islands is *bumi-putra*, or "son of the soil."

Indonesians can feel so closely tied to their villages that they do not want to move, even to other parts of Indonesia. In a program known as *transmigrasi*, the Indonesian government has tried to encourage people to move from crowded Java to other islands. Yet even with promises of open farmland, few people want to go. It must be very difficult for them to move to a new land!

Even though Indonesia has the fifth-largest population in the world and parts of it are very crowded, few Indonesians choose to live in another country. Many who do, come to the United States because they believe that they will have better opportunities for jobs and a prosperous life-style here.

Before World War II, only a few Indonesians left the country. They often came to California, where they settled down, married Americans, and became U.S. citizens. After the war, a larger number of people left Indonesia, most because they felt they could not live in the country after the Dutch had gone.

Most of the Dutch left Indonesia when it became independent because they did not feel they belonged there anymore. Although many Dutch families had lived in the islands for generations, they still carried Dutch passports. After independence, most decided to return to the Netherlands. They often were not happy in Europe, which seemed foreign to them. Many of them moved again, this time to California.

Another group that moved to the United States were the Indo-Dutch, Dutch who had married Indonesians and created a new, blended culture. These people did not consider themselves to be truly Dutch or Indonesian, and did not feel comfortable living in either country. Most settled near Los Angeles and San Jose in California. Some of them have returned—or plan to return—to Indonesia after they retire. They often miss the weather, the food, and the culture of the country in which they were raised.

When Sukarno was president, many Chinese also left Indonesia. During colonial times, the Dutch had given the Chinese special business privileges, which

Sukarno stopped. The Chinese migrated to other countries, including the United States, where they felt they would have more business opportunities.

Indonesian Students

Today, many Indonesians come to the United States to study in American universities. There are about eighteen thousand Indonesians in the United States, and more than half of them are students. Most Indonesian students do not intend to stay in the United States after graduation. Instead, they plan to return to Indonesia, where they often obtain very important positions. So many of Indonesia's politicians have studied at the University of California at Berkeley that as a group they are referred to as the Berkeley Mafia.

Although most Indonesians study in California's universities, they are beginning to enroll in schools in other states. Oregon State University now has about 150 students from Indonesia. Once a few Indonesians start to attend a school, others will follow. They usually feel more comfortable going to a place where there already are other Indonesians.

Most Indonesian students in the United States come from wealthy families, since the government cannot afford to give many scholarships. Many come from families that own businesses, and they tend to choose business majors so they can help in their family business. Computer science and engineering are other popular fields of study.

Indonesian students in the United States have formed an organization known as *Permias*, or the Indonesian Student Organization. This group helps newly arrived Indonesians adjust to American life, and also sponsors sporting and social events. In Los Angeles, Permias has one chapter for the entire city, but in San Francisco each university with an Indonesian student population has its own chapter.

An Indonesian Community

Only a small number of Indonesians choose to make the United States their home and become American citizens. The largest Indonesian community in the United States is in southern California, with about eight thousand people. They are spread out around the Los Angeles area, with many living in Loma Linda and Orange County. About 75 percent of the Indonesians in southern California are Christians, and the seventeen Indonesian churches there help newcomers adjust to the American life-style.

The Indonesian consulate has created the Indonesian Society to organize activities for Indonesians living in Los Angeles. The society sponsors lectures, cultural performances, and festivals. Each year, an Indonesian Fair is held to mark Indonesia's independence day. About a thousand people usually attend this event.

Even in the United States, Indonesians prefer to associate with members of their own ethnic group. The southern California community includes many people from Manado in northern Sulawesi. This group has established an organization called *Maesa*, which now has more than three hundred members. Maesa sponsors social activities and athletic events.

Although the Indonesian community in the United States is too small to support its own television or radio station, it does have *Pelita*, a monthly newsletter. *Pelita* is written in the Indonesian language, and mailed to two thousand readers. The twenty-page publication lists the social activities and events of the Indonesian community in southern California.

Textiles and American *Gamelan*

Probably because so few Indonesians have migrated to the United States, Indonesian influence on American culture has been limited. Many foreign cultures become known to Americans through their food, but Indonesian cooking has not yet become popular. Only a few large cities have Indonesian restaurants. Yet some Americans who are interested in art and music are beginning to learn about and appreciate Indonesian culture.

Today, many American museums and art collectors include Indonesian textiles in their collections. The country has produced few painters—except in Bali— and most of its art is textiles. Each area of Indonesia has its own style, ranging from Javanese batik to a type of weaving called *ikat*. This weaving is so complicated that it can take several years to produce one piece. In Bali, some people believe that wearing a piece of ikat will protect a person from evil. In America, many people simply enjoy hanging a piece of ikat or batik on their living-room wall for decoration.

The designs from Indonesian batik and ikat weavings are finding their way into everyday American life. They have inspired American weavers and influenced American textile manufacturers. Today, batik and other Indonesian designs can be found on sheets, pillowcases, and sofa covers.

Indonesian culture has also inspired people in the international music world. The English composer Benjamin Britten was influenced by the haunting melodies of the gamelan orchestra, especially in his opera *Death in Venice*. Lou Harrison and William Colvig, who produce modern classical music, include gamelan music in their pieces.

A few Americans have become so interested in Indonesian music and art that they have begun to practice it themselves. The members of one American gamelan orchestra, Sekar Jaya, have been playing Balinese music in the San Francisco area since 1979. In 1985, Sekar Jaya became the first foreign gamelan orchestra ever to play in Indonesia.

Several Americans have also become dalangs, or puppet masters. One, Larry Reed, has performed the wayang kulit—the shadow-puppet play—throughout the United States, Canada, Indonesia, and France. He has even adapted the techniques of wayang kulit to some Western plays.

Learning About Indonesia

Indonesia is one of the largest nations on earth, with an ancient and varied culture, yet few Americans know much about it. Although the islands are a major producer of oil and natural gas, they are no longer as important as they once were, when they were at the center of the spice trade.

To help Americans learn more about Indonesia, a group of U.S. and Indonesian organizations is sponsoring a Festival of Indonesia. The festival includes three art exhibits that will tour the United States for more than a year. One exhibit displays the arts from Java's royal palaces. Another is a collection of classical

A group of Indonesians in the United States raises the Indonesian flag as part of an Indonesian Independence Day ceremony.

Indonesian art, and the third shows the arts and crafts of the outer islands. There will also be dance performances, concerts, film and television programs, and other activities taking place throughout the country. The festival's organizers hope that Americans will gain a greater understanding of Indonesia's rich culture.

The Indonesian government is working hard to improve Indonesia's status among the world's nations. Because Indonesia has the fifth largest population in the world, many Indonesians feel that the nation should play a more important role in international affairs. Although Indonesia still faces many problems at home, it has accomplished much in the past fifty years. Indonesians hope that the country will accomplish much more in the next fifty years, and they look to the future with pride.

Appendix

Indonesian Embassies and Consulates in the United States and Canada

Indonesian consulates in the United States and Canada offer assistance to Americans and Canadians who want to understand Indonesian ways. For information and resource materials about Indonesia, contact the consulate or embassy nearest you.

U.S. Consulates and Embassy

Chicago, Illinois
Consulate of Indonesia
Two Illinois Center, Suite 1422
233 North Michigan Avenue
Chicago, Illinois 60601
Phone (312) 938-0101

Houston, Texas
Consulate General of Indonesia
5633 Richmond Avenue
Houston, Texas 77057
Phone (713) 785-1691

Los Angeles, California
Consulate General of Indonesia
3457 Wilshire Boulevard
Los Angeles, California 90010
Phone (213) 383-5126

New York, New York
Consulate General of Indonesia
5 East 68th Street
New York, New York 10021
Phone (212) 879-0600

San Francisco, California
Consulate of Indonesia
1111 Columbus Avenue
San Francisco, California 94133
Phone (415) 474-9571

Washington, D.C.
Embassy of the Republic of Indonesia
2020 Massachusetts Avenue, N.W.
Washington, D.C. 20036
Phone (202) 775-5200

Canadian Consulates and Embassy

Ottawa, Ontario
    Embassy of the Republic of In-
      donesia
    287 McLaren Street
    Ottawa, Ontario K2P 0L9
    Phone (613) 236-7404

Toronto, Ontario
    Consulate General of Indonesia
    425 University Avenue
    Toronto, Ontario M5G 1T6
    Phone (416) 591-6461

Vancouver, British Columbia
    Consulate General of Indonesia
    1455 West Georgia Street
    Vancouver, British Columbia
      V6G 2T3
    Phone (604) 682-8858

Glossary

agama (AH·gah·mah)—religion; a course that is taught in all Indonesian schools

anak (AH·nahk)—a child

Bahasa Indonesia (BAH·hah·sah IHN·doh·nee·see·ah)—the national language of Indonesia

Balinese (BAH·lih·neez)—the people who live in Bali

batik (BAH·teek)—a method of decorating fabric; a design is drawn or stamped on the fabric with hot wax, and the fabric is dipped in dye until the design appears

becak (BEH·jak)—a three-wheeled bicycle taxi

benjang (BEHN·jahng)—a western Javanese sport in which players use foot-long sticks to wrestle each other to the ground

buah hati (BOO·uh HAH·tee)—"heart's fruit" or sweetheart

bumiputra (BOO·mee·POO·trah)—"son of the soil"; the name the Indonesian people use to distinguish themselves from foreigners

bung (buhng)—brother; President Sukarno used this title to show his equality with the Indonesian people

dalang (DAH·lahng)—a puppet master; this person controls the puppets, tells the story, and directs the musicians in *wayang kulit*, the traditional shadow-puppet play

durian (DOO·ree·uhn)—a large, green, spiky fruit with a creamy white interior and an unpleasant smell

es campur (ehs CHAHM·poor)—a dish of shaved ice, coconut, cubes of gelatin dessert, pineapple, and other fruit, topped with a sweet sauce

es kelapa muda (ehs keh·LAH·pah MOO·dah)—iced coconut juice

gado gado (GAH· doh GAH· doh)—a salad made from vegetables such as potatoes, cabbage, and bean sprouts, covered with a spicy peanut sauce

Galungan (GAH·loon·gahn)—the most important Balinese festival, which takes place every 210 days

gamelan (GAH·meh·lahn)—a traditional Javanese and Balinese orchestra which includes gongs, drums, and xylophones

gasing (GAH·sing)—a game played with wooden tops in the Riau Islands

gotong royong (GOH·tuhng ROH·yuhng)—a system of mutual cooperation in which people help each other; traditional Indonesian society follows this system

guru (GOO·roo)—a teacher

Hari Raya (HAH·ree REYE·ah)—a Muslim holiday that celebrates the end of *Ramadan*, the Muslim month of fasting

Iban (EE·bahn)—a tribe that lives in the jungles of Kalimantan

ikat (EE·kaht)—a type of complicated weaving

Javanese (JAH·vah·neez)—the people who live in central and eastern Java

kamar kecil (kah·MAHR keh·CHEEL)—"the little room"; a phrase used to mean "toilet"

kampong (KAHM·puhng)—an Indonesian village

Karang Teruna (KAH·rahng teh·ROO·nah)—an Indonesian sports and social organization for young people between the ages of ten and twenty-five

Kassada (kah·SAH·dah)—a Buddhist festival in which cows and chickens are thrown into a live volcano

kebaya (kur·BY·yah)—a tight-fitting blouse worn by Indonesian women with a *sarong*

keris (keh·RIHS)—a dagger with a wavy blade, worn by Javanese men in formal dress

Koran (KOH·rahn)—the holy book of Islam

krupuk (KROO·puhk)—crunchy shrimp crackers

madrasah (mah·DRAH·sah)—a Muslim school that teaches academic subjects as well as the Islam religion

mandi (MAN·dee)—the Indonesian bathtub, a large tiled tank or barrel of water

mangosteen (MAYN·goh·steen)—a small, round fruit with a thick purple shell and sweet segments inside

mata hari (MAH·tah HAH·ree)—"eye of the day"; a phrase used to mean "sun"

merdeka (mur·DEH·kah)—freedom; this became the battle cry of the Indonesians in their struggle for independence from the Dutch

Minangkabau (MIH·nahng·KAH·bow)—the people who live in western Sumatra

nasi goreng (NAH·see GOH·rayng)—fried rice

nasi Padang (NAH·see PAH·dahng)—"Padang rice"; a restaurant that serves spicy Minangkabau food

Pancasila (pahn·CHAH·see·lah)—the philosophy which the Indonesian government tries to follow; it consists of five principles—belief in God, nationalism, democracy, humanitarianism, and justice

pasar (PAH·sahr)—a traditional Indonesian market

pencak silat (PAHN·chahk SEE·laht)—a traditional Indonesian martial art form; also called *silat*

pramuka (PRAH·moo·kah)—a scouting organization for Indonesian schoolchildren

Ramadan (RAH·mah·dahn)—the Muslim month of fasting

rijstafel (RIJ·stah·fehl)—a Dutch word meaning "rice table," used for a buffet feast with many dishes

salak (SAH·lahk)—a fruit with a brown peel that resembles a snake skin; also called a "snake fruit"

sambal (SAHM·bul)—a spicy chili sauce

sarong (SAH·rahng)—a long skirt made from batik material, worn by both women and men in Indonesia

sate (SAH·teh)—skewers of barbecued meat

sekolah dasar (seh·KOH·lah DAH·sahr)—grade school

sekolah menengah pertama (seh·KOH·lah MEH·nehn·jah pur·TAH·mah)—junior high school

sepak takraw (SEH·pahk TAH·krahw)—a sport simi-lar to volleyball, except that players use only their heads, feet, and legs to move the ball

silat (SEE·laht)—another name for *pencak silat*

sisemba (sih·SEHM·bah)—a type of kick-boxing played by the Toraja in southern Sulawesi

soto ayam (SOH·toh EYE·ahm)—chicken soup

Tanah Air Kita (TAH·nah EYE·ur KEE·tah)—"our land and water"; the name that Indonesians use for their country

tau tau (tow tow)—wooden carved images placed out-side of graves built in cliffs by the Toraja people of southern Sulawesi

Toraja (toh·RAH·jah)—a group of people who live in the mountains of southern Sulawesi

transmigrasi (TRAHNS·mee·grah·see)—an Indonesian government program that attempts to move people from crowded Java and Bali to new homes on the outer islands

upacara (OO·pah·chah·rah)—a special ceremony which takes place on Monday mornings at all Indonesian schools

warung (WAH·rung)—a roadside stall that sells cooked food

wayang kulit (WEYE·awng KOO·liht)—the traditional shadow-puppet play, popular in Java and Bali

Selected Bibliography

Alibasah, Margaret Muth. *Indonesian Folk Tales.* Jakarta, Indonesia: Penerbit Djambatan, 1986.

Aman, S. D. B. *Folk Tales from Indonesia.* Jakarta, Indonesia: Penerbit Djambatan, 1988.

Bruce, Ginny, Mary Covernton, and Alan Samagalski. *Indonesia: A Travel Survival Kit.* South Yarra, Australia: Lonely Planet Publications, 1986.

Bunge, Frederica, ed. *Indonesia: A Country Study.* Washington, D.C.: U.S. Government Printing Office, 1983.

Dalton, Bill. *Indonesia Handbook.* Chico, California: Moon Publications, 1985.

Fairclough, Chris. *We Live in Indonesia.* New York: Bookwright Press, 1984.

Index

About the Author

Judy Jacobs spent six years study-
ing, traveling, and working as a
journalist in Asia, including an
extensive period in Indonesia.
She regularly returns to Indonesia for her current position as
editor of an Asia/Pacific travel
magazine. Her articles have appeared in more than thirty publications, including *Pacific Travel
News, Asia Travel Trade, The
Christian Science Monitor*, and *Asia 2000*. This is her first book
for children.

Ms. Jacobs received her bachelor's degree in Asian Studies
from DePauw University in Indiana. She currently lives with
her husband and two children in Oakland, California.